Grade 2	Skills 6

The War of 1812

Reader

Amplify Core Knowledge Language Arts

Core Knowledge®

ISBN 978-1-61700-212-0

Printed in the USA
01 RRCV 2016

Table of Contents
The War of 1812
Skills 6 Reader

Introduction to *The War of 1812*

A New Nation: American Independence

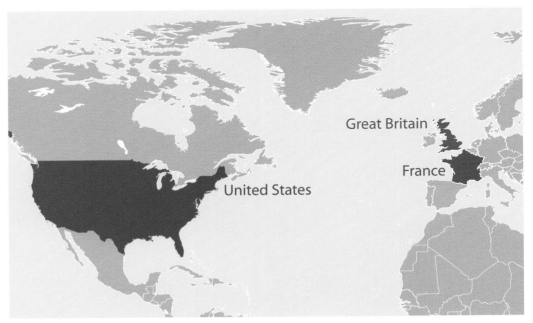

The United States, Great Britain, and France

Christopher Columbus

The Pilgrims

The Revolutionary War

3

The American Government

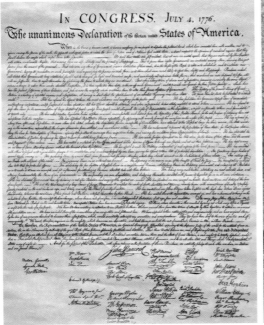

The Declaration of Independence

The Constitution

The Founding Fathers

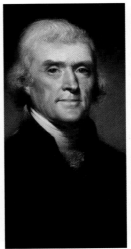

George Washington   John Adams   Thomas Jefferson   James Madison

The British Government

King George III

Where Parliament meets

Early Colonial Life

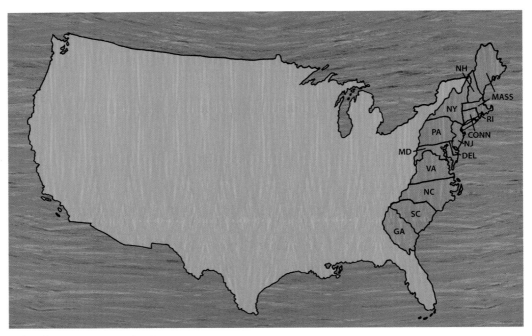

The thirteen original colonies

Colonial farmers

American port

Westward expansion

The War of 1812

USS Constitution

Modern navy ship

Cannon from the 1800s

American soldiers

Washington, D.C.

The President's House and Capitol in the 1800s

The White House and Capitol today

Chapter 1

Trouble with the British

In 1812, James Madison had a hard choice to make. Many Americans were angry with the **British**. Some of them were saying the United States should **declare war** on Great Britain. But others disagreed. They said the United States should not go to war.

Madison was president of the United States. He had to decide what to do. Should he ask the **U.S. Congress** to declare war? Or should he try to keep the **peace**?

James Madison was the fourth president of the United States.

At the time, Great Britain was already at war with France. The two countries had been fighting for years. Most of the countries in Europe were involved in the war. Some sided with the British. Others sided with the French.

The French were led by a man named Napoleon. He was a brave leader. He had beaten the British in a number of battles. Still, the British kept fighting.

The French were led by a man named Napoleon.

The United States tried to stay out of this big war. At first, most Americans did not care to get involved. American **traders** wished to trade with both Great Britain and France. But this led to problems.

When U.S. ships traded with the British, the French got upset. They did not want Americans trading with their enemies. When U.S. ships traded with the French, the British got upset for the same reason.

Sometimes British ships would stop American ships to keep them from trading with the French. Sometimes French ships would stop American ships to keep them from trading with the British.

The Americans had problems with both the French and the British. As time went on, the problems with the British increased.

King George III

GREAT
BRITAIN

Napoleon

FRANCE

The British and the French were at war.

The British had a strong **army** and an even stronger **navy**. But serving in the British Navy was a hard job. Some people quit. Others ran away. This was a problem for the British. They needed all the men they could get. How else could they **defeat** the French?

The British spent a lot of time looking for men who had run off. From time to time they would stop American ships. British officers would come on deck to look for British men. They would grab men and force them to serve in the British Navy. This was called **impressment**.

The British said they only took British men who had run away. But they were not always careful. Sometimes they grabbed Americans. Stories about men taken by the British were printed in the papers. How do you think Americans felt when they read them? They felt angry. Some of them felt the United States needed to fight back. They said the United States needed to declare war on Great Britain.

British commanders (on the right) look on as men from American ships (left) are "impressed"—forced to serve in the British Navy.

Impressment was one problem. But there were others. Many in the United States were also upset with the British for trading with Native Americans.

In 1812, most Americans were farmers. At first, most farmers had homes near the East Coast. But then the country began to grow. People went west. They settled in places far from the coast. They set up farms. They planted crops. There was just one problem: there were already people living there!

The settlers were moving onto land where Native Americans hunted and made their homes. Native Americans did not like this. There were many fights between settlers and Native Americans.

People continued the westward expansion.

The British controlled Canada. They sent traders south from Canada to trade with Native Americans. These traders sold all sorts of things to Native Americans.

The British said they had a right to trade with Native Americans. But lots of people in the United States did not see it that way. They said the British were helping Native Americans attack American settlers. They felt they needed to fight back.

You can see there were many reasons for Americans to be angry with the British. But there were also good reasons for not declaring war. A war causes death, wrecks towns, and costs a lot of money. Plus, Americans felt that the British would not be easy to defeat. President Madison and the men in Congress would have to think long and hard about declaring war.

President Madison and the men in Congress would have to think long and hard about declaring war.

Chapter 2

The War Hawks

At first, President Madison tried to keep America out of the war. He tried to make a deal with the British. He asked them to stop taking American sailors. He asked them to stop trading with Native Americans. But he did not ask Congress to declare war.

This made some people happy. There were many people in the United States who did not care to go to war. Most **merchants** and traders felt this way. Most of them had homes in the cities along the East Coast. They traded with Great Britain, as well as other countries. A war would mean less trade between countries. It would mean sunken ships and lost goods. A war would cost them money. For this reason, as well as some others, most merchants **opposed** the war.

Merchants in Boston (shown here) and other eastern cities wanted to avoid a war.

But others felt a war was needed. The states out west, like Ohio, Kentucky, and Tennessee, were closer to Native American land. The settlers in these states were scared of Native Americans. They were also angry with the British.

These people were called "War Hawks." They made loud, angry speeches. They complained about impressment. They complained that the British were selling guns to Native Americans. They felt the United States needed to declare war.

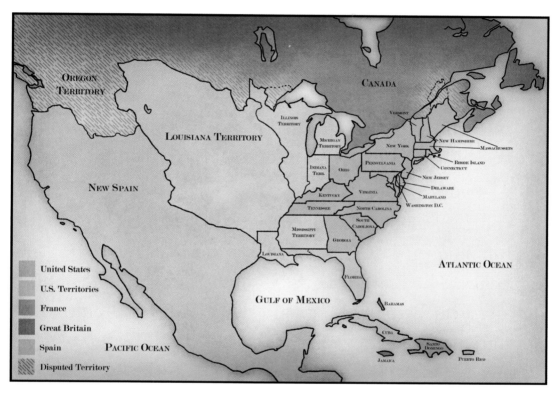

In 1812, the United States was much smaller than it is today. There were far fewer states. Many people who lived in the western states were War Hawks, who wanted to go to war with the British.

When some War Hawks found out that the British were selling guns to Native Americans, it made them angry.

These War Hawks gave President Madison an earful. They got up in Congress and made angry speeches. They said that the United States should stand up to Great Britain. They said that Madison should ask Congress to declare war.

War Hawks, like Henry Clay, made angry speeches in Congress.

Chapter 3

The War Starts

Presidents have to make hard choices. James Madison had to decide whether to side with the War Hawks or with the merchants who hoped for peace. In the end, he sided with the War Hawks. Madison asked Congress to declare war. On June 18, 1812, the United States declared war on Great Britain.

The Americans were in for a hard fight. The British had a huge army. They also had the world's biggest navy. But the British were already at war with France. They could only send some of their troops to fight the United States. That was a good thing for the Americans. It meant that the United States would have a better chance of winning.

The British were already fighting France, so they could only send some of their soldiers to fight the Americans.

Even so, not a lot of people at the time could imagine that the United States could win. Today the United States is a strong nation. It has been around for many years. It has a strong army and navy. But that was not the case in 1812.

In 1812, the United States was not very old as a country. It had broken away from Great Britain only about 30 years before.

The United States had a different kind of government, too. At the time, most of the nations of Europe were **monarchies**. That means they were ruled by kings or queens. A king or queen would rule until he or she died. Then, in most cases, the oldest son would take over. The United States was not a monarchy. It did not have a king or queen. Instead, it had a president. The president was chosen by voters. He did not get to serve until he died. He served for four years. Then the voters got a chance to pick their president. If they voted for a different president, the old one had to step down.

In 1812, most people in the world felt that the American government had a very strange way of doing things. They were not sure that the system would last and that the United States would be able to survive.

James Madison was an elected president at a time when most countries were ruled by kings and queens.

In 1812, the United States did not have a strong army. In fact, the U.S. Army was tiny. It had about 4,000 soldiers.

The navy was tiny, too. George Washington, the first president, had set it up. He didn't think the United States needed a big navy, but just a small number of ships to protect merchants from pirates.

President Madison found a way to make the army bigger. He got farmers to join. Many Americans were farmers. They used guns to hunt and to defend their homes. Madison called on these farmers. He asked them to grab their guns and join the army. Farmers were paid money and given land for joining.

The U.S. soldiers were not well trained. Still, Madison was sure they could win if they attacked the British in Canada. He sent the army north to Canada.

The attack on Canada did not go well. The army lost a string of battles. The United States lost **forts** along the border. The army was simply not ready for war.

Soldiers in the U.S. Army

No one expected much from the tiny U.S. Navy. But things went better on the seas than they did on land. The United States battled bravely. They beat the British in a number of naval battles.

American men in the navy during the War of 1812

Chapter 4

A Famous Ship

The ship on the right is the USS *Constitution*. It was one of the ships that battled in the War of 1812. The letters 'USS' stand for *United States Ship*.

The USS Constitution

The USS *Constitution* was named for a very important **document**, the Constitution of the United States. The Constitution lays out the laws of the land. It states what people serving in each **branch** of the U.S. government can do. It says what the president, the Congress, and the **Supreme Court** can do—and also what they cannot do.

James Madison had helped write the Constitution. He had also played a key role in getting states to accept it. The people of the United States were proud of the Constitution. So they named one of their fighting ships the USS *Constitution*.

A painting of the Constitutional Convention, where the U.S. Constitution was signed

During the War of 1812, the USS *Constitution* had a **string** of battles on the high seas.

In one battle, the USS *Constitution* attacked a British ship. It was a hard fight. The sailors on both sides fired cannons. The guns blazed and smoked. The two ships drifted closer. Once they even bumped into each other.

Cannonballs from the USS *Constitution* smashed into the side of the British ship. They made big holes in it. They ripped off a sail. They knocked down the ship's **masts**.

The British ship fired back. But its cannonballs did less damage to the U.S. ship. In fact, some of them bounced off the thick walls of the American ship!

When the American sailors saw this, they cheered.

"Hooray!" one of them shouted. "Her sides are made of iron!"

In fact, however, the sides of the ship were not made of iron but of very thick **planks** of wood. The wooden sides of the USS *Constitution* were much thicker than most ships.

The USS Constitution

The USS *Constitution* won the battle. The British ship was so smashed up that it could not be fixed. The British had to sink it.

When people were told about the battle, they became excited. They yelled and shouted. They waved flags and had parties. They treated the sailors on the USS *Constitution* as heroes. They also gave the ship a nickname. They called it "Old Ironsides" because its wooden sides seemed as strong as iron.

Old Ironsides kept on fighting. It battled more than twenty times and never lost a battle!

The USS Constitution *is still floating today. You can visit "Old Ironsides" in Boston Harbor.*

Chapter 5

The Attack on Washington, D.C.

In August of 1814, President Madison was upset. Two years had passed. The war was still going on. The U.S. Army had won some battles, and it had lost some battles.

The British had landed an army near Washington, D.C. British soldiers were marching. Madison hoped the U.S. Army would be able to stop them.

At the time, Washington, D.C., was a young town. Some buildings had just been finished, such as the **Capitol**. Others were not finished yet. Still, it was an important place. It was where the U.S. Congress met to make laws. It was where the Supreme Court met.

The Capitol Building in Washington, D.C., as it looked in 1810

The President's House was a special house that had been constructed for the president. (Today it is called the White House.) It was only about ten years old at the time. It was home to President Madison and his wife, Dolley.

President Madison was aware that there was going to be a big battle outside the city. He planned to go **support the troops**. He ordered some soldiers to protect Mrs. Madison and the President's House. Then he jumped on his horse and rode off.

The battle outside the city did not go well. The U.S. Army was beaten.

People quickly found out about the **defeat**. The army had lost! The British were coming! People in the city **panicked**. They grabbed their things and ran away. The roads were jammed with people and carts.

The President's House was the home of the U.S. president.

President Madison could not get back to the President's House. His wife, Dolley, was left there with servants and soldiers.

The soldiers ran away.

Mrs. Madison could not stay in the President's House. The British would be there soon. She had to **flee**.

Mrs. Madison hoped to take as much with her as she could. But which things should she take? There were many fine things in the President's House. She loved a lamp that hung in one room. But there was no way she could take that. It was too heavy. She had a big closet of fancy dresses. She loved them, too. But there were more important things for her to carry away.

Dolley Madison

In the end, Mrs. Madison left most of her own things behind. Instead, she carried away things that were important to the American people. She grabbed papers and letters. She stuffed as many of them as she could into a **trunk**.

Mrs. Madison was ready to leave. Then she remembered one last thing. It was a painting of George Washington. She did not want the painting to fall into the hands of the British. She called one of President Madison's trusted servants, Paul Jennings, for help. There was no time to take the painting gently from its frame. Jennings and the other servants broke the frame so they could quickly remove the canvas painting. They carefully rolled the canvas like a tube and carried it away.

"It is done!" said Dolley Madison. Then she ran out the door to safety.

Dolley Madison helped to save a painting of George Washington.

Chapter 6

The Burning of Washington, D.C.

The British Army marched into Washington, D.C. The British soldiers were angry because the U.S. Army had burned York, the capital city of Canada. They planned to get back at the Americans by burning the U.S. Capitol Building.

The British soldiers went to the Capitol Building. This was where the U.S. Congress met. They set it on fire. Then they marched down the hill to the President's House.

The British arrived just after Dolley Madison left. They broke down the doors and **charged** inside.

This painting shows the Capitol Building after it was set on fire by the British.

The President's House was empty. In the dining room, the table had been set for dinner.

The British general sat down with some of his men. They ate dinner. They drank some wine, too. As a joke, they **toasted** President Madison. They lifted up their wine glasses and thanked him for the wine.

After dinner, the British soldiers started smashing things. They smashed the dishes. They smashed the table. They smashed the chairs.

The soldiers ran up and down in the President's House looking for things to steal. They took the spoons and forks. They took the buckles from Mrs. Madison's shoes. They even took the love letters her husband had sent her! The house was **ransacked**.

Then the British general ordered his men to set the house on fire. The soldiers lit their **torches**. Then they went from room to room. They lit the **drapes** on fire. They burned the beds. They burned the desks and chairs. They even burned Mrs. Madison's dresses.

The British burned the President's House.

Then the British marched away. They did not care to take over the city. They just planned to burn it. Burning the city would be a **heavy blow**. The British hoped the Americans might feel like there was no longer hope and stop fighting.

Later that day a storm rolled in. The rain stopped most of the fires. But it was too late. Many of the buildings were already lost.

Later in the week, the Madisons came home. The President's House was still standing. But it was a mess. The walls were black with **soot**. The windows were broken. All of their things had been stolen or burned. They felt they would never call the President's House home again.

This image shows how the President's House looked after it was burned.

Chapter 7

The Attack on Baltimore

Washington, D.C., took ten years to construct. It took less than one day to destroy it.

Next the British planned to attack Baltimore. Baltimore was a big city north of Washington, D.C. At the time, it was the third largest city in the United States. It was also a key **port**.

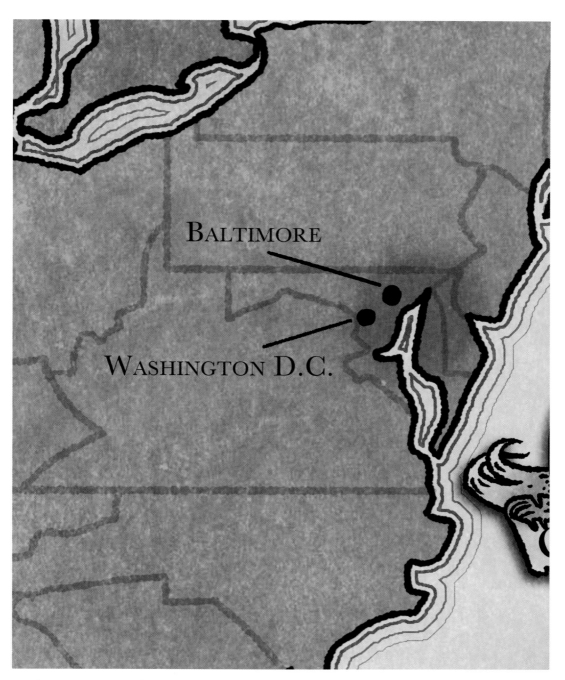

Baltimore was a big city and a key port north of Washington, D.C.

Baltimore was protected from naval attack by a large fort. It was called Fort McHenry.

The British focused on Fort McHenry. They hoped that if they could take the fort, they could take the city. They planned to attack the fort by land and also by sea.

The people of the city were aware an attack was coming. They got ready. They **piled up** supplies. They set up walls. They even sank ships in the **harbor** to keep the British ships from getting too close to the city. All of the people in the city **pitched in**. Even the children helped.

Fort McHenry as it looks today

A year earlier, the soldiers in Fort McHenry felt like they needed a flag they could fly over the fort. They asked a local woman named Mary Pickersgill to make a flag. "Make it big," they told her. "Make it so big that the British will be able to see it from miles away!"

The U.S. flag is covered with stars and stripes. Today, the U.S. flag has fifty stars and thirteen stripes. Each star stands for one of the fifty states of the United States. Each stripe stands for one of the thirteen original colonies. Sometimes America's flag is referred to as "the stars and stripes."

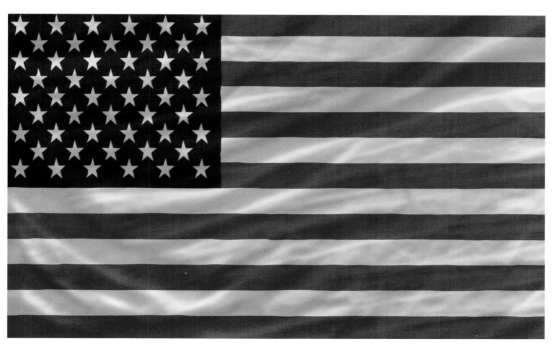

The U.S. flag today

The flag that Mary Pickersgill made for Fort McHenry was different. It had fifteen stars and fifteen stripes.

The Fort McHenry flag was different in another way, too. It was huge! Each star was two feet across. Each stripe was two feet tall and forty-two feet long.

Mrs. Pickersgill could not do all the **stitching** herself. The flag was too big. She needed help. She got her daughter to help her. But she still needed more help. She had her servants help with the stitching. Still she needed more help. She sent for two of her **nieces**. That did the trick. She and her five helpers stitched day and night until the flag was finished.

When it was done, the flag was as large as a house. It was hung on a giant pole over the fort. You could see it from miles away.

A year earlier, the soldiers at Fort McHenry asked Mary Pickersgill to make a flag to fly over the fort.

The British arrived later in the week. They sent troops to attack the city. But this time the U.S. soldiers were ready. They stopped the British Army. The British **commander** was killed during the attack.

The British went back to their ships. They decided to attack Fort McHenry with their navy instead.

A flag like Mary Pickersgill's flag flying at Fort McHenry

Chapter 8

Francis Scott Key and the National Anthem

On September 13, 1814, British ships **opened fire** on Fort McHenry. They fired **rockets** and **mortars**.

The soldiers in the fort would have fired back, but there was not much point. The guns in the fort were old. They could not hit the British ships.

The British ships kept firing for a long time. They fired all day. They fired on into the night.

This image shows the British firing on Fort McHenry from far away.

An American named Francis Scott Key watched the British attack. He was on a boat in the harbor. Key was not a soldier. He did not fight in the battle. But he was able to see it. He could see the British ships blasting away. He could see Fort McHenry. He could also see the huge flag Mrs. Pickersgill had made.

Key kept his eye on the American flag. As long as the flag was still flying at the fort, America was still in the battle. It meant that the troops in Fort McHenry had not given up. If the flag went down, that would mean America was no longer fighting. That would mean that the troops in the fort had given up.

Key watched all day. He was still watching when the sun set. He was proud that the flag was still flying.

Francis Scott Key

At night it was harder for Key to see. But there were flashes of light. Sometimes a rocket would go **streaking** through the darkness. Sometimes a bomb would explode and light up the sky. The flashes of light allowed Key to see the flag.

The firing went on until just before dawn. Then it stopped. The sun had not come up yet. It was still dark. There were no rockets blasting. There were no bombs bursting in the air. Key could not see much. The silence was puzzling. What did it mean? Was the battle over? Had the soldiers in the fort given up? Key could not tell.

Key waited nervously. At last the sun rose. Key looked at the fort. And what did he see? The soldiers had raised the huge flag that Mrs. Pickersgill had made. It was not the U.S. soldiers who had given up. It was the British sailors! They had stopped firing on the fort.

Key felt a surge of joy. He felt pride, too. The brave men in the fort had not given up!

When the sun rose on Fort McHenry, Francis Scott Key saw that the American flag was still flying.

Key felt **inspired**. He hoped to share with others what he had seen. He needed to tell what it was like to wait and wait—and then see the flag still flying in the morning. Key reached into his pocket. He found an old letter. On the back, he wrote a poem. Here is the first part of his poem:

O say can you see by the dawn's early light

*What so proudly we **hailed** at the twilight's last gleaming?*

*Whose broad stripes and bright stars through the **perilous** fight,*

*O'er the **ramparts** we watched were so **gallantly** streaming?*

And the rocket's red glare, the bombs bursting in air,

*Gave **proof** through the night that our flag was still there.*

O say does that Star-Spangled Banner yet wave

O'er the land of the free and the home of the brave?

Key did not know then that, one day, his poem would become our **national anthem**.

The U.S. flag was still flying at Fort McHenry after the attack on Baltimore.

Chapter 9
Andrew Jackson

After the Battle of Baltimore, both sides began to get tired of the war. They called a meeting. Men from both sides sat down to try to form a **peace treaty**. But in the meantime, the war went on.

The British sent troops to attack the city of New Orleans, on the Gulf of Mexico.

New Orleans

You can see why New Orleans is an important place if you look at the map on the next page. The city is located at the **mouth** of the Mississippi River, right where the river drains into the Gulf of Mexico. From New Orleans you can travel north along the Mississippi River. You can also turn off onto other rivers that feed into the Mississippi, like the Ohio River. These rivers are like highways that lead right into the middle of North America.

In 1814, New Orleans was already an important, big port. Lots of ships landed there. Farmers could ship their goods down the river and sell them in New Orleans. Traders could unload goods in New Orleans and ship them up the river. New Orleans was an important city, not only for the people who had homes there, but also for the farmers up the river in places like Ohio and Kentucky.

If the British took New Orleans, they could control trade along the Mississippi. Farmers in Ohio and Kentucky would be cut off. The Americans could not let this happen. They sent an army to defend the city. The army was led by a man named Andrew Jackson.

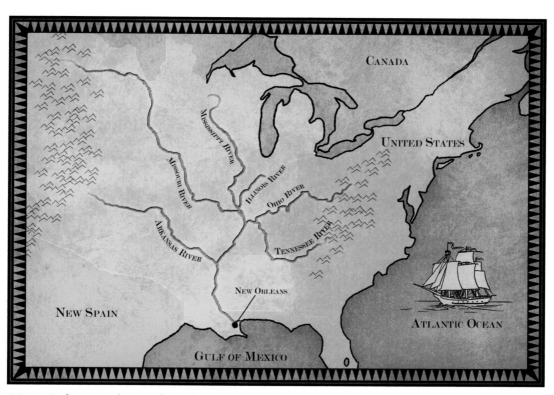

New Orleans is located at the mouth of the Mississippi River.

Andrew Jackson was from Tennessee. He had joined the U.S. Army during the American Revolution. At the time he was just a boy. He was too young to fight. He carried notes from place to place.

During the Revolution, Jackson and his brother were taken prisoner by the British. It was a difficult time for them. They were treated badly. They almost starved to death. Jackson's brother got sick and died.

While he was a prisoner, Jackson had a run-in with a British officer. The man ordered Jackson to clean his boots. Jackson was proud and stubborn. He refused. The man shouted at Jackson. Still Jackson refused. The man struck Jackson with his weapon. Jackson was left with a scar on his face.

As a result of this, Andrew Jackson had no love for the British. He was happy to fight them again as an army **general** when the War of 1812 broke out.

Andrew Jackson

Jackson had not been trained as a soldier. But he was bold and strong. His mother had died when he was young. He had gotten by on his own as an **orphan**. He had made his own way in life.

During the first part of the War of 1812, Jackson battled against Native Americans in the west. Many Native Americans had sided with the British.

Jackson's men called him "Old **Hickory**" because he was as strong as a **knotty** old piece of hickory wood. In 1814, "Old Hickory" was given an important job. He was told to raise an army to protect New Orleans. Jackson rushed to the city. He picked up new troops along the way. Many of the men who joined him were farmers. But there were also free African Americans, Native Americans, and even pirates. When Jackson arrived, he ordered his **ragtag** army to set up walls and get ready for an attack. Then they waited.

Andrew Jackson on horseback

Chapter 10

The End of the War

On January 8, 1815, the British attacked New Orleans. They planned on winning without much trouble. But they did not know how brave Andrew Jackson and his men were—or how good they were with their weapons.

The British soldiers had on bright red coats. A wave of them charged. Jackson's men crouched behind their walls. They took careful aim. Then they fired. Their bullets hit the first wave of British soldiers.

The British kept coming. Jackson and his men kept firing. The wall helped to keep them safe. When it was all over, the U.S. flag was still flying. The British gave up their attack.

Andrew Jackson (with the sword) and his soldiers defended New Orleans from attack by the British.

The British took heavy losses. Two thousand of their men were killed or hurt. The U.S. Army lost no more than one hundred men. New Orleans was safe! Americans cheered for Andrew Jackson and the Battle of New Orleans.

After time passed, a letter arrived. It said that the war was already over. On December 24, 1814, the United States and Great Britain had signed a treaty to end the war. This was two weeks before the Battle of New Orleans! But Jackson and his men did not know that.

In those days news traveled slowly. There were no radios or television sets. There were no phones. There were no computers to send emails. A letter could only travel as fast as the man who carried it. It took a couple of weeks for news of the treaty to get from Europe to the United States. That is why Jackson and his men did not find out about the treaty until after the battle. America's greatest victory in the War of 1812 came after the war was already over!

The Battle of New Orleans

The War of 1812 lasted three years. It's hard to say who won. Both sides won battles. The British burned Washington, D.C. But the Americans won the Battle of New Orleans. "Old Ironsides" won a number of battles on the sea. But other U.S. ships were sunk. All in all, there was no clear winner.

It might seem as if the war was for nothing. But some things had changed. The Americans had battled together as a nation, and they had done it well. They had taken on the mighty British and had held their own. The world saw they were strong.

The end of the war marked the start of a new age in U.S. history. It was an age of national pride. The War of 1812 showed that the United States of America was here to stay.

Andrew Jackson went on to become the seventh president of the United States. His face appears on the twenty-dollar bill.

Chapter 11

Our National Anthem

A national anthem is a special **patriotic** song. Many countries have a national anthem. People sing a national anthem to show that they are proud of their country.

In the United States, our national anthem is "The Star-Spangled Banner." The words to this song were written by Francis Scott Key during the War of 1812. The song describes what Key saw during the attack on Fort McHenry.

After the attack, he saw the U.S. flag, or in his words, the "star-spangled banner."

An old poster about "The Star-Spangled Banner"

We sing "The Star-Spangled Banner" before baseball games and other sporting events. We sing it on holidays like the Fourth of July. We sing it on special days when we gather together. Sometimes we sing it at school. We sing it to show that we care about our country.

In the United States, we always stand when we sing or hear the national anthem. If you are playing or talking and you hear this song, you should stop what you are doing and turn to face a flag. You may wish to place your right hand over your heart. You should stand still and look at the flag until the song is over. You should never talk or giggle or fool around during the national anthem.

One way to show respect for the flag is to place your right hand on your heart.

During the national anthem, you will see men taking off their hats. You may also see soldiers **saluting** the flag. They salute by bringing their right hand up to their head or the tip of their hat. Also, the flag should never touch the ground. These are all ways of showing respect for the U.S. flag and pride in our country.

This soldier is saluting the American flag.

You know that "The Star-Spangled Banner" was written by Francis Scott Key. But did you know that it was not always our national anthem? In fact, it took more than one hundred years for it to become our national anthem.

When it was first written, "The Star-Spangled Banner" was not a song. It was a poem. A little later, people took the words and set them to music. They sang the words to a tune that was popular at the time. Do you ever change the words to songs you know? That's what people did with "The Star-Spangled Banner." They took an old tune and gave it different words.

Soon, lots of people were singing "The Star-Spangled Banner." It was a big hit!

This image shows deaf students singing—and signing—"The Star-Spangled Banner." It was taken in Ohio around 1920.

"The Star-Spangled Banner" became a popular national song. People all over the nation liked to sing it. But they also liked to sing lots of other songs, and we still sing some of them today. Do you know "Yankee Doodle"? What about "My Country, 'Tis of Thee"? Have you ever sung "America, the Beautiful"? These are all patriotic songs that we sing to show how we feel about our country.

If you went to a big **state dinner** at the White House one hundred years ago, the band might have played "The Star-Spangled Banner." Or it might have played "Yankee Doodle," or "My Country, 'Tis of Thee." At that time, the United States did not have a national anthem. It had a set of national songs. Then, in 1931, Congress made "The Star-Spangled Banner" the national anthem.

"The Star-Spangled Banner" is sung to show that we love our country. It is one of the things that unite us as a people. So when you sing it, sing it with pride!

Until 1931, the United States did not have a national anthem. It had lots of patriotic songs.

Chapter 12

Making Sense
of the National Anthem

Francis Scott Key wrote "The Star-Spangled Banner" almost two hundred years ago. There are some old words in the poem. Some parts can be hard to understand. Let's look at the words and try to make sense of them.

On the next page is the first verse of the song, the part that we sing before a sporting event. Can you read it two or three times?

"O'er" is a short form of the word *over*.

O say can you see by the dawn's early light

What so proudly we hailed at the twilight's last gleaming?

Whose broad stripes and bright stars through the perilous fight,

O'er the ramparts we watched were so gallantly streaming?

And the rocket's red glare, the bombs bursting in air,

Gave proof through the night that our flag was still there.

O say does that star-spangled banner yet wave

O'er the land of the free and the home of the brave?

The first verse of "The Star-Spangled Banner"

To make sense of the "The Star-Spangled Banner," it helps to think of what Francis Scott Key was doing the night he wrote it. Key was watching the attack on Fort McHenry. In the poem he describes the attack as a "perilous fight." That means it was a dangerous battle.

During the battle, Key kept his eye on Fort McHenry. In the poem he mentions the ramparts, or walls, of the fort. But what Key talks about the most is the U.S. flag that he could see flying over the fort.

Key says the flag is "spangled," or dotted, with stars. He also talks about its "broad stripes." When the wind blows, Key says these stripes blow back and forth. They look like they are "streaming" or rippling in the air. Have you ever seen a flag look that way?

When the U.S. flag blows in the wind, its stripes appear to stream and ripple like waves.

In the poem, Key describes three different times when he looked for the flag. First, he tells us he looked for the flag at "the twilight's last gleaming," or just as the sun set. Since it was not dark yet, Key could see. He saw that the flag was still flying over the fort. That was good. It means that the troops had not given up.

Key tells us he also looked for the flag at night. You might think he would not be able to see much at night. But Key explains that the "rocket's red glare" and the "bombs bursting in air" lit up the night sky. These flashes of light helped him see. They gave him "proof" that the flag was still flying.

Key looked for the flag again just before dawn. This time he could not see it. Remember, the attack on the fort had stopped just before dawn. There were no more "bombs bursting in air." There was no more "rocket's red glare." It was dark. Was the flag still flying? Had the troops in the fort given up? Or had the British? In the time before the sun rose, Key did not know. At that time, he had a lot of questions, but not a lot of answers.

Key looked for the flag three times — "at the twilight's last gleaming," at night, and then "by the dawn's early light."

Look back at the words Key wrote. Do you see the question marks? There are three of them. An important thing to understand about our national anthem is that it starts with a set of questions.

In the first lines, Key asks a question:

"O say can you see by the dawn's early light What so proudly we hailed at the twilight's last gleaming?"

Wow! That's a long sentence. Suppose we broke it up into shorter sentences and used simpler words. Then it might sound like this: "The sun is coming up. Tell me, my friend, can you see the flag? Remember? We saw it last night at sunset. Now the night has passed. Is it still there?"

In the last lines of the song, Key asks another question. He says,

"O say does that star-spangled banner yet wave
O'er the land of the free and the home of the brave?"

The "star-spangled banner" is the American flag. "The land of the free and the home of the brave" is what Key calls his country. It's another name for the United States. So Key is really asking the same thing he asked before. He is asking, "Is our flag still waving?"

Key asks these questions, but it might seem like he never answers them. In fact, he does. If you ever get a chance to read the rest of the poem, you will see that Key answers his own questions a little later. There is a part later in the poem where he says, "Yes! The flag is still flying! Hooray!" But that is in a part of the poem that we don't sing very much. Most of the time we only sing the part with the questions. We don't sing the part with the answers.

So the next time you sing or hear the national anthem, think of Francis Scott Key. Think of him watching the bombs bursting over Fort McHenry. Think of him checking on the flag and wondering if it's still flying. If you keep your eyes on the flag during the song, you will be doing just what Francis Scott Key was doing that night long ago.

On the shore dimly seen through the mists of the deep
Where the foe's haughty host in dread silence reposes,
What is that which the breeze, o'er the towering steep,
As it fitfully blows, half conceals, half discloses?
Now it catches the gleam of the morning's first beam,
In full glory reflected now shines in the stream,
'Tis the star-spangled banner — O long may it wave
O'er the land of the free and the home of the brave!
And where is that band who so vauntingly swore,
That the havoc of war and the battle's confusion
A home and a Country should leave us no more?
Their blood has wash'd out their foul footstep's pollution.
No refuge could save the hireling and slave
From the terror of flight or the gloom of the grave,
And the star-spangled banner in triumph doth wave
O'er the land of the free and the home of the brave.
O thus be it ever when freemen shall stand
Between their lov'd home and the war's desolation!
Blest with vict'ry and peace may the heav'n rescued land
Praise the power that hath made and preserv'd us a nation!
Then conquer we must, when our cause it is just,
And this be our motto — "In God is our trust,"
And the star-spangled banner in triumph shall wave
O'er the land of the free and the home of the brave.

The rest of Francis Scott Key's poem

Chapter 13

Dolley Madison

Dolley Payne Madison was the wife of the fourth president of the United States, James Madison. The president's wife is called the First Lady. Dolley Madison was one of the most famous First Ladies in history.

Dolley Madison was born Dolley Payne in 1768. She had four brothers and three sisters. When she was a little girl, she and her family had a very simple life. They belonged to the Quaker church. Quakers believed in living simply. They went to plain **meeting halls** instead of fancy churches. They ate plain food.

Dolley had a strict **upbringing**. She was not allowed to sit with the boys in church or in school. She was not allowed to dance or play cards.

A Quaker meeting around 1790

When she was young, Dolley Payne loved books. She liked going to school. She had lots of friends. She loved the color yellow. She hoped to get a nice yellow dress, but her parents said no. They were Quakers, and they did not believe in fancy dresses.

When Dolley Payne was an adult, she married a man named Mr. Todd. They had a little boy. They were married only for a little while. Then Mr. Todd got yellow fever and died.

Mrs. Todd was a **widow**.

People told James Madison about Dolley. They said she was smart and **charming**. He was eager to meet her. Madison was not president at the time. But he was already an important person. He was very smart and serious.

James Madison was much older than Dolley Todd. He was also shorter than her. But she liked him anyway. She even had a funny nickname for him. She called him the "Great Little Madison."

Soon James Madison asked Dolley Todd to marry him. She had to think about this because he was not a Quaker. But, in the end, she said yes.

Dolley Madison

James Madison

The Madisons were happy together. Dolley was a great help to her husband. When he was president he had to host fancy state dinners for visitors. Dolley helped him. She was a charming **hostess**. She welcomed all sorts of visitors to the President's House. There were **diplomats** and visitors from **distant** lands. There were Native American chiefs. Dolley Madison always served her ice cream. At that time, ice cream was something new. Lots of people had never tasted it before.

When the British marched into Washington, D.C., during the War of 1812, Dolley Madison was very brave. She stayed in the President's House as long as she could. Before she left, she grabbed many important papers. She even helped to save a painting of George Washington.

Dolley Madison entertaining visitors at the President's House

Glossary

A

anthem—an important song

army—a group of soldiers trained to fight on land

B

branch—one of three major parts of the government

British—people who are from Great Britain

C

Capitol—the building in Washington, D.C., where Congress meets

charge—to rush into (**charged**)

charming—pleasing or delightful

commander—a high-ranking officer in the military

D

declare war—to officially say that one country will start a war with another country (**declaring war**)

defeat—loss in a contest or battle

diplomat—a person who represents his or her country (**diplomats**)

distant—far away

document—an official or important paper

drape—curtain (**drapes**)

F

flee—to run away from danger

fort—a large building constructed to survive enemy attacks (**forts**)

G

gallantly—impressively

general—a high-ranking officer in the military

H

hail—to greet or see (**hailed**)

harbor—an area of calm, deep water near land, where ships can safely put down their anchors

heavy blow—a difficult loss to deal with

hickory—a tree with very hard wood

hostess—a woman who entertains guests at an event

I

impressment—the state of being forced to serve in the British Navy (**impressed**)

inspired—wanting to do something

K

knotty—having many dark marks on wood where branches once grew

M

mast—the tall pole on a ship to which the sails are attached (**masts**)

meeting hall—an indoor space where many people can gather (**meeting halls**)

merchant—a person who sells things (**merchants**)

monarchy—a government ruled by a king or queen (**monarchies**)

mortar—a type of cannon (**mortars**)

mouth—the place where a river enters the ocean

N

national—relating to a nation or country

navy—a group of soldiers trained to fight battles at sea on board ships

niece—the daughter of your brother or sister (**nieces**)

O

open fire—to shoot a weapon in order to start a fight or battle (**opened fire**)

oppose—to be against something (**opposed**)

orphan—a child whose parents are no longer alive

P

panic—to suddenly become very scared (**panicked**)

patriotic—having or showing support and love for your country

peace—a state of no war or fighting

perilous—dangerous

pile up—to collect (**piled up**)

pitch in—to help with (**pitched in**)

plank—a long, thick board (**planks**)

port—a place on the water near land, where ships load and unload cargo

proof—something showing that something else is true or correct

R

ragtag—disorganized and made up of many different types

rampart—the wall of a fort (**ramparts**)

ransack—to search in order to steal and cause damage
(**ransacked**)

rocket—a type of missile (**rockets**)

S

salute—to show respect (**saluting**)

soot—the black powder left behind when something burns

state dinner—a special dinner hosted by the president of the
United States for important people (**state dinners**)

stitching—sewing (**stitched**)

streak—to move quickly (**streaking**)

string—a series

support the troops—to provide encouragement and
sometimes food and supplies to soldiers

Supreme Court—the highest court of law in the United
States

T

toast—to raise a glass and drink in honor of someone or something (**toasted**)

torch—a piece of wood that burns at one end (**torches**)

trader—someone who exchanges something to get something in return (**traders**, **traded**, **trading**, **trade**)

treaty—a formal agreement between countries

trunk—a large box or crate used to carry things

U

upbringing—the way a child is raised

U.S. Congress—the people elected to make laws for the United States

W

widow—a woman whose husband has passed away

About this Book

This book has been created for use by students learning to read with the Core Knowledge Reading Program. Readability levels are suitable for early readers. The book has also been carefully leveled in terms of its "code load," or the number of spellings used in the stories.

The English writing system is complex. It uses more than 200 spellings to stand for 40-odd sounds. Many sounds can be spelled several different ways, and many spellings can be pronounced several different ways. This book has been designed to make early reading experiences simpler and more productive by using a subset of the available spellings. It uses *only* spellings students have been taught to sound out as part of their phonics lessons, plus a handful of Tricky Words, which have also been deliberately introduced in the lessons. This means the stories will be 100% decodable if they are assigned at the proper time.

As the students move through the program, they learn new spellings and the "code load" in the decodable Readers increases gradually. The code load graphic on this page indicates the number of spellings students are expected to know in order to read the first story of the book and the number of spellings students are expected to know in order to read the final stories in the book. The columns on the opposite page list the specific spellings and Tricky Words students are expected to recognize at the beginning of this Reader. The bullets at the bottom of the opposite page identify spellings, Tricky Words, and other topics that are introduced gradually in the unit this Reader accompanies.

Visit us on the web at www.coreknowledge.org.

Code Knowledge assumed at the beginning of this Reader:

VOWEL SOUNDS AND SPELLINGS:

/i/ as in _it_, m_y_th

/e/ as in b_e_d

/a/ as in h_a_t

/u/ as in b_u_t, s_o_n, c_o_me, t_ou_ch

/o/ as in h_o_t

/ae/ as in c_a_ke, p_a_per, w_ai_t, d_ay_, h_ey_

ee/ as in b_ee_, funn_y_, b_ea_ch, cook_ie_, k_ey_, Pet_e_

/ie/ as in b_i_te, b_i_ting, tr_y_, t_ie_, n_igh_t

/oe/ as in h_o_me, _o_pen, sn_ow_, b_oa_t, t_oe_,

/ue/ as in c_u_te

/aw/ as in l_aw_, P_au_l, c_augh_t

/oo/ as in s_oo_n

/oo/ as in l_oo_k

/ou/ as in sh_ou_t, n_ow_

/oi/ as in _oi_l, t_oy_

/er/ as in h_er_, h_ur_t, b_ir_d

/ar/ as in c_ar_

/or/ as in f_or_

/ə/ as in _a_bout, ben_e_fit

CONSONANT SOUNDS AND SPELLINGS:

/p/ as in _p_ot, pe_pp_er

/b/ as in _b_at, ru_bb_ing

/t/ as in _t_op, mi_tt_, mark_ed_

/d/ as in _d_og, sle_dd_ing, hogg_ed_

/k/ as in _c_at, _k_id, so_cc_er, ba_ck_

/g/ as in _g_et, bi_gg_er

/ch/ as in _ch_op, i_tch_

/j/ as in _j_et, _g_em, lar_ge_

/f/ as in _f_at, sni_ff_

/v/ as in _v_et, twel_ve_

/s/ as in _s_it, mi_ss_, _c_ent, rin_se_, prin_ce_

/z/ as in _z_ip, bu_zz_, dog_s_

/th/ as in _th_in

/th/ as in _th_em

/m/ as in _m_an, swi_mm_ing

/n/ as in _n_ot, ba_nn_er, _kn_ock

/ng/ as in so_ng_, pi_nk_

/h/ as in _h_ot

/w/ as in _w_et, _wh_en

/l/ as in _l_ip, fi_ll_

/r/ as in _r_ed, fe_rr_et, _wr_ist

/y/ as in _y_es

/sh/ as in _sh_ip

/x/ as in ta_x_

/qu/ as in _qu_it

/ə/ + /l/ as in app_le_, shov_el_, penc_il_, nav_al_

/sh/ + /ə/ + /n/ as in ac_tion_

TRICKY WORDS:

a, again, against, all, are, be, before, break, bridge, building, by, could, death, do, down, eyes, father, friend, from, ghost, go, have, he, how, I, me, my, no, of, one, once, people, said, says, she, should, so, some, street, sure, the, there, their, they, to, two, you, your, walk, was, water, we, were, what, where, who, why, wizard, word, would

ABBREVIATIONS AND SYMBOLS:

Mrs., Mr.

Code Knowledge added gradually in the unit for this Reader:

- Beginning with "Introduction to The War of 1812": /f/ as in _ph_one
- Beginning with "Trouble with the British": Tricky Words _Great Britain, Europe, native, Americans, signature_
- Beginning with "The War Hawks": /er/ as in act_or_
- Beginning with "The War Starts": /e/ as in h_ea_d, Tricky Words _imagine, soldier, Washington_
- Beginning with "A Famous Ship": Tricky Word _Ironsides_
- Beginning with "The Attack on Washington, D.C.": Tricky Word _special_
- Beginning with "The Burning of Washington, D.C.": Tricky Word _shoe_
- Beginning with "The Attack on Baltimore": Tricky Word _Fort McHenry_
- Beginning with "Francis Scott Key and the National Anthem": /er/ as in doll_ar_, /ee/ as in sk_i_, Tricky Words _early, whose, broad, bomb_
- Beginning with "Andrew Jackson": Tricky Words _Andrew, new_
- Beginning with "Dolley Madison": /k/ as in _sch_ool

Core Knowledge Language Arts

Series Editor-in-Chief

E. D. Hirsch, Jr.

President

Linda Bevilacqua

Rights Manager

Elizabeth Bland

Editorial Staff

Mick Anderson
Robin Blackshire
Laura Drummond
Emma Earnst
Lucinda Ewing
Sara Hunt
Rosie McCormick
Cynthia Peng
Liz Pettit
Tonya Ronayne
Deborah Samley
Kate Stephenson
Elizabeth Wafler
James Walsh
Sarah Zelinke

Design and Graphics Staff

Kelsie Harman
Liz Loewenstein
Bridget Moriarty
Lauren Pack
Cecilia Sorochin

Consulting Project Management Services

ScribeConcepts.com

Additional Consulting Services

Erin Kist
Carolyn Pinkerton
Scott Ritchie
Kelina Summers

Acknowledgments

These materials are the result of the work, advice, and encouragement of numerous individuals over many years. Some of those singled out here already know the depth of our gratitude; others may be surprised to find themselves thanked publicly for help they gave quietly and generously for the sake of the enterprise alone. To helpers named and unnamed we are deeply grateful.

Contributors to Earlier Versions of these Materials

Susan B. Albaugh, Kazuko Ashizawa, Kim Berrall, Ang Blanchette, Nancy Braier, Maggie Buchanan, Paula Coyner, Kathryn M. Cummings, Michelle De Groot, Michael Donegan, Diana Espinal, Mary E. Forbes, Michael L. Ford, Sue Fulton, Carolyn Gosse, Dorrit Green, Liza Greene, Ted Hirsch, Danielle Knecht, James K. Lee, Matt Leech, Diane Henry Leipzig, Robin Luecke, Martha G. Mack, Liana Mahoney, Isabel McLean, Steve Morrison, Juliane K. Munson, Elizabeth B. Rasmussen, Ellen Sadler, Rachael L. Shaw, Sivan B. Sherman, Diane Auger Smith, Laura Tortorelli, Khara Turnbull, Miriam E. Vidaver, Michelle L. Warner, Catherine S. Whittington, Jeannette A. Williams

We would like to extend special recognition to Program Directors Matthew Davis and Souzanne Wright who were instrumental to the early development of this program.

Schools

We are truly grateful to the teachers, students, and administrators of the following schools for their willingness to field test these materials and for their invaluable advice: Capitol View Elementary, Challenge Foundation Academy (IN), Community Academy Public Charter School, Lake Lure Classical Academy, Lepanto Elementary School, New Holland Core Knowledge Academy, Paramount School of Excellence, Pioneer Challenge Foundation Academy, New York City PS 26R (The Carteret School), PS 30X (Wilton School), PS 50X (Clara Barton School), PS 96Q, PS 102X (Joseph O. Loretan), PS 104Q (The Bays Water), PS 214K (Michael Friedsam), PS 223Q (Lyndon B. Johnson School), PS 308K (Clara Cardwell), PS 333Q (Goldie Maple Academy), Sequoyah Elementary School, South Shore Charter Public School, Spartanburg Charter School, Steed Elementary School, Thomas Jefferson Classical Academy, Three Oaks Elementary, West Manor Elementary.

And a special thanks to the CKLA Pilot Coordinators Anita Henderson, Yasmin Lugo-Hernandez, and Susan Smith, whose suggestions and day-to-day support to teachers using these materials in their classrooms was critical.

Core Knowledge Language Arts

Editorial Staff

Susan Lambert, Vice President, CKLA
Rachel Wolf, Editorial Director
Sarah McClurg, Senior Content Specialist
Elizabeth Wade, PhD, Managing Curriculum Developer
Patricia Erno, Senior Curriculum Developer
Jamie Raade, Senior Curriculum Developer
Marc Goldsmith, Curriculum Developer
Carrie Hughes, Curriculum Developer
Amber McWilliams, ELL Specialist
Brian Black, Managing Copy Editor

Project Management

Matthew Ely, Senior Project Manager
Jennifer Skelley, Senior Producer
Cesar Parra, Project Manager

Design and Graphics Staff

Todd Rawson, Design Director
Chris O'Flaherty, Art Director
Carmela Stricklett, Art Director
Stephanie Cooper, Art Director
Annah Kessler, Visual Designer
Erin O'Donnell, Senior Production Designer
Tim Chi Ly, Illustrator
John Starr, Illustrator

Contributors

Ann Andrew
Desirée Beach
Leslie Beach
Nicole Crook
Stephen Currie
Kira Dykema
Carol Emerson
Jennifer Flewelling
Mairin Genova
Christina Gonzalez Vega
Stephanie Hamilton
Rowena Hymer
Brooke Hudson
Jason Jacobs
Leslie Johnson
Debra Levitt
Bridget Looney
Christina Martinez
Julie McGeorge
Evelyn Norman
Leighann Pennington
Heather Perry
Tim Quiroz
Maureen Richel
Jessica Richardson
Carol Ronka
Laura Seal
Cynthia Shields
Alison Tepper
Karen Venditti
Carri Waloven
Michelle Warner

Core Knowledge

Credits

Every effort has been taken to trace and acknowledge copyrights. The editors tender their apologies for any accidental infringement where copyright has proved untraceable. They would be pleased to insert the appropriate acknowledgment in any subsequent edition of this publication. Trademarks and trade names are shown in this publication for illustrative purposes only and are the property of their respective owners. The references to trademarks and trade names given herein do not affect their validity.

All photographs are used under license from Shutterstock, Inc. unless otherwise noted.

Writers

Mike Sanford, Core Knowledge Staff

Illustrators and Image Sources

Cover: Library of Congress, Prints & Photographs Division, NYWT&S Collection, LC-DIG-ds-00032a; 1: Library of Congress, Prints & Photographs Division, NYWT&S Collection, LC-DIG-ds-00032a; 2 (top): Shutterstock; 2 (bottom): Library of Congress, Prints & Photographs Division, LC-DIG-pga-02388 ; 3 (top): Shari Griffiths; 3 (bottom): Library of Congress, Prints & Photographs Division, LC-DIG-pga-00995; 4 (top left): Shutterstock; 4 (top right): Shutterstock; 4 (bottom left): original by Gilbert Stuart; 4 (bottom center left): original by John Trumbull; 4 (bottom center right): original by Rembrandt Peale; 4 (bottom right): original by John Vanderlyn; 5: Library of Congress, Prints and Photographs Division, LC-USZ62-97721; 5 (inset): Shutterstock; 6 (top): Core Knowledge Staff; 6 (bottom): Sharae Peterson; 7 (top): Simini Blocker; 7 (bottom): Simini Blocker; 8 (top): USS Constitution vs Guerriere by Michel Felice Corne (1752-1845). Image courtesy of the Beverley R. Robinson Collection, U.S. Naval Academy Museum; 8 (bottom): Shutterstock; 9 (top): Shutterstock; 9 (bottom): Library of Congress, Prints & Photographs Division, LC-DIG-pga-01891; 10 (top): Library of Congress, Prints and Photographs Division, LC-DIG-ppmsca-09502; 10 (bottom): Library of Congress, Prints & Photographs Division, LC-DIG-ppmsca-07708; 11: Shutterstock; 13: original by John Vanderlyn15; Shutterstock17: Jacob Wyatt; 19: Library of Congress, Prints and Photographs Division, LC-USZ62-75535 ; 21: Simini Blocker; 23: Library of Congress, Prints and Photographs Division, LC-USZ62-16960; 25: Simini Blocker; 27: Erika Baird; 29: original by Matthew Harris Jouett; 31: Scott Hammond; 33: original by John Vanderlyn; 35: Library of Congress, Prints and Photographs Division, LC-USZC4-4419; 37: Library of Congress, Prints and Photographs Division, LC-USZC4-4419; 39: James Lemass/James Lemass/SuperStock; 41: Signing of the Constitution, by Howard Chandler Christy. Courtesy of Architect of the Capitol; 43: USS Constitution vs Guerriere by Michel Felice Corne (1752-1845). Image courtesy of the Beverley R. Robinson Collection, U.S. Naval Academy Museum; 45: Shutterstock; 47: Library of Congress, Prints & Photographs Division, LC-DIG-ppmsca-07708; 49: Library of Congress, Prints and Photographs Division, LC-DIG-ppmsca-09502; 51: original by Gilbert Stuart; 53: Courtesy of The Montpelier Foundation, William Woodward, artist, 2009; 55: Library of Congress, Prints and Photographs Division, LC-DIG-ppmsca-23076; 57: Department of Defense. Department of the Army. Office of the Chief Signal Officer. (09/18/1947 - 02/28/1964); 59: Library of Congress, Prints & Photographs Division, LC-DIG-ppmsca-23757; 61: Erika Baird; 63: Shutterstock; 65: Shutterstock; 67 (inset): Library of Congress, Prints and Photographs Division, LC-DIG-hec-04302; 67 (flag): original by National Star-Spangled Banner Centennial, Baltimore, Maryland, September 6 to 13, 1914; 69: National Park Service; 71: Library of Congress, Prints and Photographs Division, LC-DIG-ppmsca-35544; 73: Library of Congress, Prints & Photographs Division, LC-USZ62-53017; 75: Library of Congress, Prints & Photographs Division, NYWT&S Collection, LC-DIG-ds-00032a; 77: original by National Star-Spangled Banner Centennial, Baltimore, Maryland, September 6 to 13, 1914; 79: original by William Bennett; 81: Erika Baird; 83: Library of Congress, Prints and Photographs Division, LC-USZC4-6466; 85: Library of Congress, Prints & Photographs Division, LC-USZC4-6221; 87: Library of Congress, Prints & Photographs Division, LC-USZC4-6221; 89: Library of Congress, Prints & Photographs Division, LC-DIG-pga-01838; 91: Shutterstock; 93: Library of Congress, Prints & Photographs Division, LC-DIG-ppmsca-31279; 95: Shutterstock; 97: Shutterstock; 99: Library of Congress, Prints & Photographs Division, LC-DIG-npcc-33373; 101 (flag): Shutterstock; 101 (top left): Library of Congress, Music Division, LC-USZ62-91855; 101 (top middle): Library of Congress, Prints and Photographs Division, LOT 10615-12; 101 (top right): Library of Congress, Music Division, LC-USZ62-91874; 101 (bottom left): Library of Congress, Music Division, LC-USZ62-91870; 101 (bottom right): Library of Congress, Music Division, LC-USZ62-91851; 103: Shutterstock; 105: Shutterstock; 107: Jacob Wyatt; 109: Jacob Wyatt; 111: Jacob Wyatt; 113: Shutterstock; 115: Gracechurch Street Meeting, 1770s, artist unknown; 117 (top): original by Gilbert Stuart; 117 (bottom): original by John Vanderlyn; 119: Library of Congress, Prints & Photographs Division, LC-USZC4-6138